The Great Stones of England

Photographs by Homer Sykes

WEIDENFELD AND NICOLSON

LONDON

INTRODUCTION

Shrouded in mystery, romanticized for centuries, objects of unabated scholarship and conjecture, the magnificent stones that dot England's landscape are a window to its prehistoric past. Set in some of the most spectacular scenery in the country, these great monuments never cease to provide a rich source of wonderment, inspiration and mysticism. While many are now popular tourist attractions or located precariously close to busy roads, and despite their decay and natural erosion, these megaliths retain a dignity and beauty that span millennia.

Some of these haunting structures date as far back as the

Neolithic period – 4500 to 2000 BC – the remains of which we see today in the numerous henge monuments and long barrows like those in and around Avebury. The Bronze Age – 2000 to 750 BC – saw the evolution of stone circles, of which Stonehenge is the best known, and a number of other strange phenomena – holed stones, menhirs – that show the evidence of human workmanship and give rise to a number of fascinating theories about their use. Though many of these stones were standing by the time the Romans arrived in England and were associated with pagan rituals, many of the legends that have been handed down to us come from zealous Christian cults that adopted them in an attempt to abolish the pagan rites and to integrate them into their own religious beliefs.

Archaeologists have tried hard to explain some of the mysteries of these massive assemblages – How were they moved? What do their configurations signify? What can be learned from them today? – but the secret of their true meaning remains largely unanswered. And, indeed, it is their inexplicable nature that ensures the power of these great stones will never fade.

WEST KENNETT AVENUE

MEANDERING from the Sanctuary on Overton Hill to the circles of Avebury in an area dense with Neolithic sites, this 'street' dating to around 2300 BC and made up of some one hundred paired stones was most likely used for ceremonial purposes.

Chun Quoit

Cornwall is home to a number of ancient sites, and in the moorland near Morvah stands a poetic example of the potent simplicity of megaliths. In this Neolithic ensemble a large slab, almost ten feet square and over two feet thick, is delicately balanced on three stones.

DEVIL'S ARROWS

IT is not clear what or who has given these aligned menhirs at Boroughbridge, Yorkshire, the curious grooving at the top of their towering shapes, the largest standing over twenty-two feet in height. Their name comes from a legend that tells of the stray arrows of an angered devil landing on this site.

Roche's Rock

Nestled into an outcrop of rocks in Roche, Cornwall, a ruined fourteenth-century hermitage eloquently suggests the stories surrounding it, from the dying leper kept alive here by his devoted daughter to a Cornish murderer who sought refuge among the ruins.

HOLED STONES

HOLED stones induce a lot of speculation. These four, made of granite and in a field of beautiful heather near the village of Tregeseal in Cornwall, lie in a landscape that enhances their mystery.

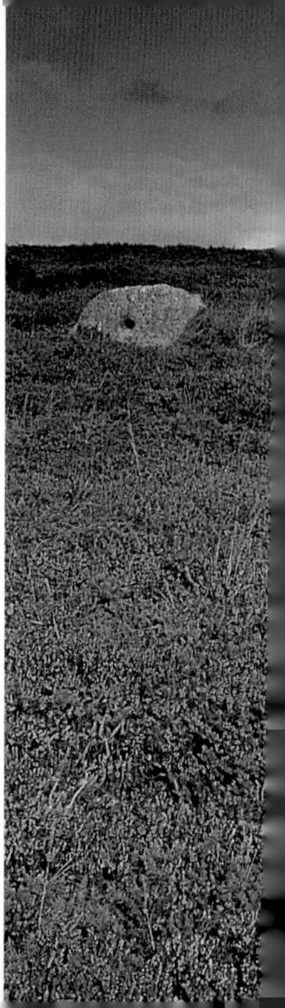

The Pipers

ONE of two menhirs located near the Merry Maidens, these tall, seemingly chiselled stones – both over thirteen feet in height – are spaced a hundred yards apart, an indication that at one time there may have been numerous other such megaliths in the area between them.

MERRY MAIDENS

NEAR Lamorna in Cornwall is a circular array of granite stones, comparatively small but showing signs of human workmanship. The name of the monument probably derives from an ancient legend spun by the Christians, who, keen to curb pagan rituals, turned these merry girls to stone.

STONEHENGE

THE most famous prehistoric monument in the entire world stands proudly next to a busy main road near Amesbury in Wiltshire. Its great myth has been chronicled by many over the centuries, but no one has adequately conveyed the sense of its mystery. Only by seeing it can one perceive its timeless power.

Castlerigg

In a dramatic setting near Derwent Water in Cumbria's Lake District stands a stone circle, which like many other such circles was reputedly men turned to stone. Used since Neolithic times, the circle appears to have an entrance (left). Within the circle is a small rectangle of smaller stones.

Blind Fiddler

Not far from Land's End in Cornwall, near the top of Tregonebris Hill, stands a solitary menhir, eleven feet tall. Ancient lore has it that the Bronze Age monument was once a person who was turned to stone.

MEN-AN-TOL

A MENHIR seen through another of Cornwall's many enigmatic holed stones. It doesn't take a vivid imagination to realize how these stones were used in conjunction with each other in fertility rites.

Nine Maidens

NEAR the bustling port of Penzance on Cornwall's southern coast is a stone circle that was once part of a triple circle. Legend holds that a group of maidens were turned to stone while dancing on the plains.

The Cheesewring and Druid's Chair

THIS natural rock formation of granite slabs appears to be a man-made creation. Ancient legend, in fact, relates its precarious existence to Druids, while the local folklore of today continues the mystical tales.

Lanyon Quoit

Dating back to around 4000 BC, this astonishing balancing act of huge stones has a capstone that weighs more than thirteen tons. It is hard to imagine from the photograph that one can easily (if daringly) walk under the massive assemblage.

Trethevy Quoit

The sheer height of this Neolithic burial tomb in Cornwall, a daunting fifteen feet, is a powerful reminder of the remarkable feat of positioning these enormous stone slabs in such a way that that they still stand thousands of years later. Though one has toppled into an antechamber, six still stand strong.

Scorhill Stone Circle

ONE of the more impressive stone circles in Devon is this group, which comprises some twenty stones and whose outline appears almost intact. It is thought that some of the stones, like the triangular one in the foreground, may have been laboriously carved by human hands.

Quinta Stonehenge

STONE circles have caught the imagination of many people, some so much so that they felt their estate would not be complete without a prehistoric monument on it. This one, built by Richard West according to his idea of a Celtic temple, was constructed in the nineteenth century.

NINE STONES

The brooding landscape of Devon, beneath the summit of Belstone Tor, provides the backdrop for a stone circle near the village of Belstone. It is believed that the stone circle may have surrounded a place used for burials.

Holed Stone

In an unlikely location behind a cottage in Cornwall is a holed stone that stands seven feet tall. Though little is known about these holed stones, it is thought that perhaps this one once had associations with fertility rituals.

MITCHELLS FOLD

THIS megalith from an almost perfectly formed stone circle, quarried from the nearby Stapley Hill, dates back to the beginnings of the Bronze Age. Not far from the Shropshire village of Chirbury, the circle contains only fifteen of what was probably once twice that many stones.

Avebury Stone Circles

THE significance of this group of stone circles in Wiltshire is often dwarfed by nearby Stonehenge, but the power of this massive complex never ceases to astound. Originally made up of three circles, with some megaliths weighing up to sixty tons, only a proportion now remains.

SHOVEL DOWN

THIS long Bronze Age double stone row in Devon's mysterious Dartmoor region may have once guided funereal processions to burial sites, but like many of the area's stone circles, little is known today about what function they actually served.

WAYLAND'S SMITHY

IN Uffington, Oxfordshire, is a fine Neolithic burial mound that was given its present name by the Saxons. It was used during two different periods: the original chamber dates back to around 3000 BC and a tomb built 1700 years later covered the first.

TWO SISTERS

THE foggy mist so common in Cornwall enfolds these two eleven-foot-tall solitary menhirs. It is not difficult to imagine that these were two revellers playing in the fields before they were petrified by disapproving deities.

Acknowledgements

First published in Great Britain in 1994 by George Weidenfeld and Nicolson Ltd
Orion House, 5 Upper St Martin's Lane, London WC2H 9EA

British Library Cataloguing-in-Publication Data
A catalogue record for this book is available from the British Library

Cover and series design by Peter Bridgewater/Bridgewater Book Company
Series Editor: Lucas Dietrich

Some of the material in this book was drawn from, among other sources, the Country Series volume Mysterious Britain *by Homer Sykes.*